# THE
# WATERFORD & TRAMORE
# RAILWAY

*by*

*THE LATE H. FAYLE and A. T. NEWHAM*

DAVID & CHARLES · NEWTON ABBOT

0 7153 5518 X

First edition 1964
Second edition 1972

© 1964, 1972 H. FAYLE and A. T. NEWHAM

Set in 10 on 11pt Pilgrim
and printed in Great Britain
by W J Holman Limited  Dawlish
for David & Charles (Publishers) Limited
South Devon House  Newton Abbot  Devon

# Contents

# *Illustrations*

ILLUSTRATIONS

## ACKNOWLEDGMENTS

The authors are grateful for permission to use photographs as follows:

Mr H. C. Casserley, plates 1, 3, 6, 7, 8, 9, 27, 28, 29; Mr W. B. Connell, plates 2, 12, 13; Mr R. N. Joanes, plates 5, 14; Mr R. N. Clements, plate 25; Messrs R. Y. Pickering Ltd (per Dr E. M. Patterson), plate 30.

The remainder of the photographs are taken from the authors' collection.

# CHAPTER I

# Early History

The Waterford & Tramore Railway was unique, for right up to the close of its independent existence in 1925 the rolling stock and methods of working had varied little during 70 years. Quite unconnected physically with the other Irish railways, it carried on a prosperous but somewhat retiring existence dependent almost entirely on the seaside passenger traffic between the city of Waterford and that most typical of Irish resorts, Tramore. The name is a corruption of the Gaelic 'Traigh Mhor', the 'great strand', and certainly this title was apt, for Tramore possesses one of the finest strands in Ireland, some three miles of firm sand reaching out a considerable distance when the tide is low, and providing safe and excellent bathing.

The bay in which it stands is bounded by the two rocky promontories of Brownstown Head on the east, and Great Newtown Head on the west, the latter being commonly known as The Metal Man from the iron figure of a seaman which surmounts one of three white pillars. These, with two similar but figureless pillars on Brownstown Head, serve as navigational marks to distinguish Tramore Bay from Waterford Harbour.

Seas run high at times, and the promenade has been swept away more than once; the main part of the town, which has a population of about 3,000, straggles up the hill at the west side of the bay, as owing to inundations of the sea very little building is possible on the east side. This part consists of a long narrow peninsula, known as the Burrows, with a passageway, once navigable, leading to a second strand, known as the 'back strand', consisting of pools of stagnant water and, in places, dangerous quicksands.

This 'back strand' has been continually spreading, but in the 1840s a William Malcolmson, the Quaker owner of some large spinning mills at Portlaw, 12 miles from Waterford, spent the greater part of his fortune in an attempt to dam the channel and reclaim the land. The effort was ineffectual, and no further steps were taken, so that the sea is in a fair way now to breach the narrow peninsula separating the 'back' and front strands nearer the town. In 1910 the racecourse, which adjoined the 'back strand', had to be removed to the upper part of the town. For many years Tramore was the principal watering place in the South of Ireland, mainly patronised by the citizens of Waterford, Clonmel and the neighbouring towns, and today is one of Ireland's most popular resorts.

The first attempt to provide Tramore with a railway was on 26 August 1846 when the Cork & Waterford Railway was incorporated to provide a line connecting those two cities, passing through Youghal and Dungarvan, and following the coast to within a short distance of Tramore, which was to be reached by a branch. The gauge was of course the standard Irish of 5 ft 3 in.

The length of the line was 78 miles 8 chains, with branches 19 miles 16 chains to Fermoy and Tramore, and the capital £1,000,000.

The Cork & Waterford Railway Company was soon in financial difficulties, and by 1850 the chairman announced that although nothing had been built, no less than £64,000 had been spent since the formation of the company. Because of its inability to get started on its intended line, the people at the Waterford end set to and arranged to build the Waterford & Tramore section as a separate company. The response was rapid and in less than three months a provisional committee had been formed for the purpose, the chairman being William Peet, and the secretary S. Harvey, with an office at 55 The Quay, Waterford. The accommodation was provided free, as Harvey owned the premises.

The following month, July, a prospectus was issued, the capital proposed being £90,000, and the length of the line 7¼ miles. The committee comprised no less than 13 persons, including William Peet, and was headed by the Earl of Huntingdon, the only member of the local landed gentry to support the scheme. The other members, mostly business and professional men, were: J. Barry (Tramore), B. Graham, G. Hartford, M.D., P. Kiely, Wm. Lloyd, R. W. Cherry, H. White (all of Waterford), J. Gilman, T. Blood (Dublin), and T. Moore (Kingstown).

The bill for the construction of the line was duly promoted in the British Parliament, and passed on 24 July 1851, and the capital was reduced to £48,000 in 4,800 shares of £10 each, and £10,000 preference stock, with loans totalling £19,350—in all £77,350.

Meanwhile the ground had been surveyed and found to be com-

(1) *Waterford Manor station, September* 1929
(2) *Exterior of Waterford station* 1959

(3) *No. 3 leaving Waterford, September 1929*
(4) *Waterford Manor station*
(5) *Waterford Manor station, looking towards Tramore, September 1960*

(6) & (7) *Two views of* GSR *No.* 483 *at Waterford in the early* 1930s
(8) *The same engine near Tramore, June* 1932

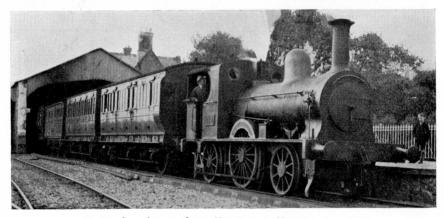

(9) *Another picture of* GSR *No. 483 near Tramore, June 1932*
(10) *Leaving Tramore, 1929*
(11) *Train in Tramore station, ex* GS & W *and* WTR *coaches*

paratively level, apart from a slight descent into Tramore, and the cost of construction was estimated at £5,500 a mile, which was considered very reasonable. Amongst those who walked the site of the line in August 1851 were Sir James Dombrain, and Mr Le Fanu, the engineer-in-charge, the former becoming the first chairman of the constituted company. Born in Canterbury, England, in 1793, he was for 20 years connected with the coastguard service as Inspector-General, and his association with the railway sponsors followed his retirement. Le Fanu had surveyed and built many Irish railways, and continued to practise as a civil engineer until his appointment as a Commissioner of Public Works.

The contract for the construction was awarded to the well-known contractor, William Dargan, and the arrangement was, to say the least, unusual as Dargan was not only to build the line but also to acquire the necessary land.

The total price was fixed at £41,500, and Dargan was prepared to accept bonds for any balance due to him. It would appear that he acquired a substantial number of shares in the new undertaking, as the *Waterford News* of 5 December 1856 states that Joseph Malcolmson, Esq. had purchased 1,400 shares of £10 each previously held by William Dargan since the construction of the line. The preference stock was mainly issued to Dargan in payment for the work.

Dargan speedily began the building of the line, the first sod being cut on 10 February 1853, and although at first hampered by bad weather, resulting in only three miles being laid by the following May, the railway was completed and ready for opening by 2 September 1853.

Three days later came the official opening, when the directors and 200 guests travelled to Tramore and back, the single journey taking 25 minutes. Apparently they were highly pleased with all they saw, as a second run was made before the company adjourned for a banquet.

The trial trip was pronounced satisfactory, and it was stated that no time would be lost in inaugurating the public service. This started the following day, the line having previously been inspected by Lt. Tyler, R.N., Inspecting Officer to the Board of Trade. The first train, consisting of an engine and first-class coach, left the Waterford terminus at 12 noon for Tramore, the journey taking 18 minutes. On the return run, however, a slight hitch occurred: the locomotive came suddenly to a halt and reversed a few yards. It then went on its way normally to Waterford. In the afternoon the

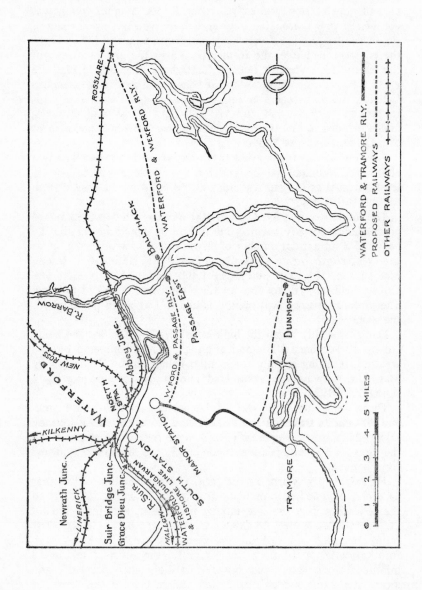

3 p.m. down train, after proceeding a short distance, had to put back for adjustments. An engineer at the time expressed the opinion that the engines were of a feeble and inferior type, which was not surprising as they were second-hand Bury type, 2—2—2 well-tanks of 1837-38 vintage.

Two days later, 1,000 persons travelled over the line, and such was the crush for the 7.30 p.m. train that police had to prevent too many travellers from boarding it. From contemporary accounts we learn that at this period only four passenger vehicles were in use, others being on order.

During the year 2,000 shares were allotted to the moribund Cork & Waterford Railway Company—which had to appoint special trustees to take charge of them—as a *quid pro quo* for the use of part of the latter's projected route between Waterford and Tramore, and as a reward for not opposing the Tramore line's bill in Parliament.

By August 1853 a 'managing conductor' had been appointed to take charge of the Waterford terminus, and by the end of the year an extension was being planned to Dunmore East, 6½ miles east of Tramore, which would have left the original line about a mile from Tramore. Dunmore is a small watering place near the mouth of Waterford Harbour, and it was hoped that a steam packet service to Great Britain might be started from here; but the harbour, though better than that at Tramore, was found to be unsuitable.

Difficulty in obtaining the land free of charge, and the desire of the Dunmore people to keep their resort 'select', caused the abandonment of the scheme; it was proposed again on later occasions, but it was as well for the Tramore Company that it was not constructed, for it would have involved signalling and other expenses not necessary on the Tramore line and would have subtracted some of the Tramore traffic. The preliminary expenses incurred by the provisional committee, £296 10s 0d, were divided between the Waterford, Dungarvan & Lismore Railway and the Waterford & Tramore Railway, and William Dargan the contractor.

In 1862 an Act was obtained for a railway from Waterford to Passage East, 9½ miles, from a junction at Ballytruckle, half a mile from the Waterford terminus of the Tramore company; the capital was £80,000 in shares and £26,000 in loans. It was proposed to run a steam ferry across the river Suir, here over half a mile wide, to Ballyhack, on the opposite side, whence another company, the Waterford & Wexford Railway, was to construct a line to Wexford and Greenore (later Rosslare). The Passage company had powers to

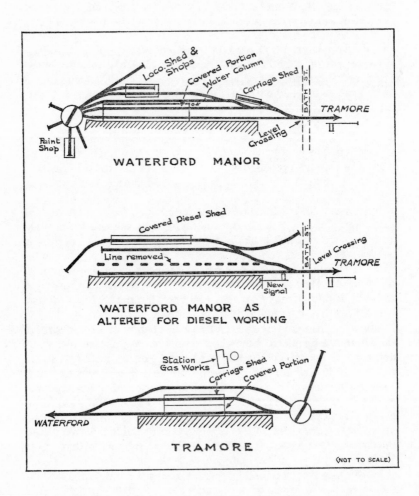

lay an additional line of rail from Ballytruckle into the Waterford terminus of the Tramore line on terms to be arranged.

The scheme, however, came to nothing, and no construction was undertaken on the Waterford side of the river. The Waterford & Wexford Railway was little more successful, the only portion built being from Greenore Harbour to Wexford, which was worked by the Dublin, Wicklow & Wexford Railway for a few years, before being taken over in 1894 by the Fishguard Bay Railway & Pier, afterwards the Fishguard & Rosslare Railways & Harbours.

Another scheme which never had Parliamentary consent concerned an extension of the Tramore line at Waterford to link with the railways on the north bank of the Suir, involving a long bridge over the river, which would have interfered with shipping. There was also a plan for a line round the south side of Waterford to join up with the Waterford, Dungarvan & Lismore Railway, which had been opened in 1878 to a terminus on the south side of the Suir, known as Waterford South.

Yet despite all the schemes and ideas, the Tramore Railway remained unconnected with other Irish railways to the close of its existence.

# WATERFORD AND TRAMORE RAILWAY.

## TIME AND FARE TABLE.

*On and after Wednesday the 7th day of September, 1853.*

TRAINS will run until further Notice, under the following Rules and Regulations:—

PASSENGERS to ensure being booked, should be at the Company's Stations at least FIVE MINUTES earlier than the time set forth in the following Tables, as the Doors of the Booking offices will be CLOSED PUNCTUALLY at the hours mentioned in these Tables; after which no person can be admitted.

RETURN TICKETS will be issued, but these will only be available for the day they are dated and issued for.

*Week Day Trains down from and up to Waterford.*

|       | 1 | 2 | 3 | 4 | 5 | 6 | 7 | 8 | 9 | 10 |
|-------|---|---|---|---|---|---|---|---|---|----|
|       | a m | a m | a m | a m | p m | p m | p m | p m | p m | p m |
|       | h m | h m | h m | h m | h m | h m | h m | h m | h m | h m |
| Down  | 7 0 | 9 0 | 10 15 | 11 15 | 1 0 | 3 0 | 4 0 | 6 0 | 7 0 | 9 0 |
| Up .. | 8 30 | 9 30 | 10 45 | 11 45 | 1 30 | 3 30 | 4 30 | 6 30 | 7 30 | 9 30 |

*Sunday Trains down from and up to Waterford*

|       | 1 | 2 | 3 | 4 | 5 | 6 | 7 | 8 | 9 |
|-------|---|---|---|---|---|---|---|---|---|
|       | a m | a m | a m | p m | p m | p m | p m | p m | p m |
|       | h m | h m | h m | h m | h m | h m | h m | h m | h m |
| Down  | 9 0 | 10 0 | 11 0 | 2 0 | 3 0 | 4 0 | 6 0 | 7 0 | 9 0 |
| Up .. | 9 30 | 10 30 | 11 30 | 2 30 | 3 30 | 4 30 | 6 30 | 7 30 | 9 30 |

## FARES:

1st Class Single Ticket......8d.    Return Ticket....1s.
2nd do.    do..............6d.    Do. do......9d.

Children under 3 years of age travel free; over 3 and under 12 years of age, at half price.

Dogs Three Pence each.

Parcels Up to 14lbs...............................3d.
     Over 14lbs. and up to 56lbs............6d.
     Over 56lbs. and up to 112lbs..........9d.

Packages above this weight, of all kinds, will be considered, and charged for as goods, viz:—
     Over 112lbs. and under 10 cwt........1s.
     Over 10 cwt. and up to 1 ton..........2s.

Luggage—1st Class passengers allowed free, 112lbs 2nd Class do. do. 84lbs.

Extra Luggage will be charged for at parcels' rates.

Articles of Merchandize cannot be considered as personal baggage; and will be charged for at parcels' rates.

Smoking, in the Carriages or at the Stations, is strictly prohibited, under a penalty, by act of parliament.

The Company's Servants are most distinctly forbidden to receive any gratuities from passengers, under pain of dismissal.

Passengers are strongly recommended to have their names and addresses plainly marked, and fastened on their luggage, and to satisfy themselves that it is placed on the train, as the Company will not hold themselves responsible for luggage, unless it is booked and paid for, according to its declared value.

By Order,
**LEWIS S. DEMAY,**
Manager-in-Chief.

Waterford, 1st September, 1853.            [s9-1t]

# CHAPTER II

# Locomotives

William Dargan, the contractor responsible for building the line, also provided the rolling stock for the first few months. For this purpose he acquired three 2—2—2 well-tank engines of Bury pattern, originally built in 1837 as 2—2—0 tender engines for the London & Birmingham Railway. Mr E. Craven, in the *Irish Railway Record Society Journal No. 26*, gives the following information : it may be recalled that the London & Birmingham Railway became the Southern Division of the London & North Western Railway.

No ex-London & Birmingham engines were sold by the LNW direct either to Dargan or to the W & T Railway, but in June 1852 William Fairbairn agreed to take ten old engines in part exchange for new ones he was building, and there can be no doubt that the three Burys used by Dargan on the W & T were three of these.

There is a note in the LNW minutes of four old engines being re-numbered 27, 191, 198, 199 in June 1852 before being sold to Fairbairn. So it seems certain that 191, which is said to have been the maker's number of one of the Tramore engines, was the last LNW (Southern Division) number.

There is an unfortunate gap in the evidence at this point, but 191 must have been one of the five engines of which one was built by the Haigh Foundry (8/37), three by Mather Dixon (10/37, 12/37 and 4/38), and one by Hawthorn (11/37). It therefore follows that the W & T Burys were not actually built by Bury at all, though they were of course made to his drawings. All these engines had been rebuilt at Wolverton in the summer of 1850 from 2—2—0 tender to 2—2—2 well tank. They had cylinders 12 in. x 18 in., driving wheels 5 ft 6 in. diameter, and heating surface 464 sq. ft.

Apparently the engines were not in too good condition, for an entry in the minute book dated 28 October 1853 states :

One of the engines with only four carriages, after being assisted up the bank from Tramore, stuck at the second bank ... and had to send back for a pilot engine. I do hope our new engines will be with us soon; all three of our present stock positively require at the moment to be in the shed.

During the following year, 1854, the company obtained a 16 in. engine from Fairbairn, which is referred to as the 'large engine', and possibly was of the 0—4—2 tender type. It was only at work pending the arrival of two tank engines, which had been ordered from the same firm, and was eventually handed back to Fairbairn in 1855, the sum of £175 being paid for its use. It is unlikely that this engine was actually returned to Fairbairn; quite probably it went to Dargan for disposal.

It was decided on 1 December 1854 'that the 13 in. cylinder engine now on the line be retained, and that Mr Dargan be paid for it, and for the use of the other engines, the sum of £1,500'. The engine in question was one of the 2—2—2 well-tanks, and probably new cylinders had been put in by Fairbairn when altering it to the 5 ft 3 in. gauge. The fact of the engine having new cylinders, and perhaps other more extensive repairs as well, would account for it being retained by the W & T when the other two, presumably 12 in. engines, were returned to Dargan.

The dimensions recorded are scanty—cylinders 13 in. x 19 in., driving wheels 5ft 7 in., leading and trailing wheels 4 ft and boiler pressure 100 lb. per sq. in. This figure would refer to the new boiler —with large bell-mouthed brass dome on the first ring—put in in 1867, when new motion was fitted as well. For this and the next class, 19 in. stroke is often quoted, but is definitely wrong in the latter case and almost certainly in both. For the boiler tracings had to be made and tenders obtained as, even at this date, this remarkable old engine which became No. 4 was of obsolete type. It retained the Bury features, including the domed firebox, throughout its career, and was used intermittently for light traffic, mainly in the winter. In September 1906 it was said to be 'incapacitated through age, and not worth repairing'. After remaining at Waterford for some years in case it might find its way to some railway museum, it was finally scrapped in 1912.

The first of the two new tank engines, contracted by Fairbairn at £3,785, appears to have gone into service in May 1855, and the second in June. They were of the 2—2—2 well-tank type, and carried the numbers 55 and 56. (As Fairbairns built about 400 engines from 1839 to 1862 and in any case did not quote numbers on their plates, it is hardly possible that these were their works numbers at this date.)

Originally they had weatherboards only, and bell-mouthed brass domes on the front boiler ring; they were numbered 1 and 2 in the company's stock, but this may have been a little later, as a reference in February 1859 states: 'The green engine being found in a bad state of repair, Fairbairn to be written to about their bad workmanship.' Later in 1859 new tubing was supplied to the engine 'which is now in better order than when it left the manufacturers. The cylinders are now 13½ in. and it can take 14 loaded carriages, when new it could not draw ten.' This was probably No. 1. The Fairbairns got new boilers, with bell-mouthed dome on the front ring, in 1865-6, but plate 18 shows that they were still without brakes then.

They were rebuilt in 1895 and 1897 respectively with larger boilers and cabs (the backsheets were added about 1907); the Avonside Engine Co. supplied these, also new bunkers and tanks. Steam brakes were fitted. Dimensions were: cylinders 13 in. x 18 in., wheels 5 ft and 3 ft 6 in., wheelbase 6 ft 6 in. + 6 ft 6 in., boiler barrel 3 ft 9 in. max. outside x 9 ft 3 in. barrel, pitched at 6 ft 2 in. and with 113 tubes 2 in. dia.; grate area 11¼ sq. ft, weight about 260 tons (adhesive 12 tons). By 1925 No. 2 was working at 125 lb. pressure. No. 1 got another similar boiler from Hawthorn Leslie in 1924, designed for 150 lb. pressure but worked at 130 lb. only. In May 1857 the company asked the Waterford & Kilkenny Railway if it had a tank engine for sale. Doubtless the W & T knew what engines were on that company's books and had an eye on one of the Tayleur 4—2—0Ts of 1848. Apparently a negative answer was received, for in September 1857 estimates were invited for the supply of a fourth engine, and in December the tender of Sharp, Stewart & Co. was accepted at £2,370. The locomotive in question was Sharp's No. 1070 of 1858, a 2—2—2 well-tank with cylinders 15 in. x 22 in., and driving wheels 5 ft 6 in. This was to have had Beattie's coal-burning firebox and feedwater-heater; to have kept such a boiler in repair would have been almost impossible for the WTR.

It is not clear at what stage, or why, the company did not accept it; Sharp's order book simply has the note 'repudiated', whilst the WTR minutes, after recording the order, never refer to it again. Possible reasons are inadequate clearance for outside cylinders, or realisation of the problems of maintenance of the Beattie boiler. However, this engine was later completed as Sharp's 1228 and became the Waveney Valley Railway's *Perseverance*. Consequently in November 1860 it was decided to order another new engine, and Slaughter, Gruning & Co. (later the Avonside Engine Co.) of Bristol delivered an 0—4—2 well-tank, their number 452, in September 1861, which became No. 3 in the company's books. Like Nos. 1 and 2, this engine had a weatherboard only, but was rebuilt at Waterford in June 1893 with a proper cab, most probably the material being supplied by the Avonside Engine Co.; a backsheet was added about 1910.

The dimensions were: cylinders 15 in. x 21 in.; coupled wheels 5 ft, trailing wheels 3 ft 6 in.; boiler barrel 3 ft 11 in. diameter x 9 ft 9¼ in. long; length of firebox 3 ft 9 in.; pressure 125 lb. per sq. in.; weight adhesive 22 tons, total 30 tons; tractive effort at 85 per cent 8,365 lb. The engine is stated to have been less satisfactory than the first two, the valves having too much lap.

The company had no need to order another engine for 46 years! It may be asked why even four engines were necessary when only one was in service except on special occasions. The answer is that the w & t's workshop resources were very limited, and two engines were generally in shop for overhaul. Indeed the locomotive superintendent seems to have done much of the skilled work, as an entry of March 1877 reads: 'Waugh's salary increased to £3 5s in consideration of his training an apprentice without fee and doing the necessary work for the company without employing other skilled labour.' Being isolated from other railways, it was not possible to borrow an engine at times of pressure.

On the withdrawal of No. 4 in 1906, some of the large Irish railways were approached with a view to obtaining a light engine secondhand, but nothing suitable was available, so the tender of Andrew Barclay & Co. was accepted for an 0—4—2 tank, the price being about £2,500. This engine was Barclay's No. 1137, and was delivered in 1908, being numbered 4 in the company's stock. It was to the maker's design, and had the following dimensions: cylinders 15 in. x 22 in.; coupled wheels 4 ft 6 in.; trailing wheels, fitted with Cartazzi axleboxes, 3 ft; wheelbase 14 ft equally divided; boiler barrel 4 ft 1⅞ in. x 9 ft 11¾ in. long; length of firebox 4 ft; 180 tubes of 1¾ in. diameter; heating surface 845 sq. ft (tubes) plus 73 sq. ft (firebox), total 918 sq. ft; grate area 12 sq. ft; pressure 160 (later 150) lb. per sq. in.; tank capacity 550 gal.; coal 12 cwt; weight empty 28 tons, loaded 32½ tons (later given as 37½ tons); tractive effort at 85 per cent 11,690 lb.; the vacuum brake was also fitted. It may be noted that the firm of Barclay built only 11 engines in all for Irish owners, of which only one other was standard gauge and nine were of various narrow gauges.*

On the amalgamation in 1925 the company's four engines, two 2—2—2WT and two 0—4—2WT, were taken over by the Great

* Fayle quotes 12 engines: 6 standard gauge and 6 turf burners for Bord na Mona.

Southern Railways and renumbered 483 to 486 in their stock. Engine No. 484 (ex-No. 2) was withdrawn from service in October 1926, and was scrapped at Waterford. Only about two months before scrapping, it had a new firebox and tubeplates, and was painted grey. No. 485 (No. 3) was scrapped in 1930, after a crank axle broke. However, the boiler was probably the deciding factor as it was handed over in 1924 with a note 'new boiler required'.

The GSR provided another locomotive to take its place. This was an ex-Midland Great Western Railway 0—6—0T, numbered 560, built by Kitson in 1893, makers' number 3527. On the MGW it had been classed E, being one of 12 engines built for work on light branches, and having the following dimensions: cylinders 15 in. x 22 in.; coupled wheels 4 ft 6 in.; wheelbase 6 ft 3 in. + 7 ft = 13 ft 3 in.; boiler barrel 4 ft diameter x 8 ft 9¾ in. long; 125 tubes of 1¾ in.; heating surface 535 (tubes) + 72 (firebox) = 577 sq. ft; grate area 13.1 sq. ft; working pressure 150 lb. per sq. in.; tanks 700 gal.; coal 1¾ tons; weight in working order, 35 tons 7 cwt; tractive effort, at 85 per cent, 11,690 lb. It proved so popular that two similar engines were afterwards sent to Waterford, No. 555, built by Sharp, Stewart & Co. in 1890, makers' No. 3694 in 1936, replaced the Tramore's 483 (ex-No. 1) which was scrapped after the derailment at Carriglong, and in 1941 No. 553, Kitson's No. 3371 of 1891, replaced the last Waterford & Tramore engine No. 486 (ex-No. 4) which was scrapped that year.

All three engines were taken to the Manor station by working them down to the disused Waterford South station, where a siding still remains, and then laying lengths of rail on the public road for about 1¾ miles; these were taken up when the engine passed over under its own steam. The operation took the best part of a Sunday. There was a short spur line leading from the turntable at the Manor station to the square outside same, by which the transfer took place.

Because of the restricted clearances, the steps on the engines were reversed to face inwards. The cabs were also altered by bringing the back to the back of the bunker. This brought them into line with the W & T engines for the benefit of the coalmen who always carried their baskets on to the footplate as the platform was too low to permit emptying direct into the bunker.

With the advent of the railcars in the autumn of 1954, all three lay in a siding at Waterford, being removed in August 1955. Nos. 553 and 555 were scrapped but 560 was sent to Cork for repair and then to Tralee for working the Fenit branch, lasting until 1963.

B

## EARLY NUMBERING AND COLOURS

The early numbering of the Waterford & Tramore engines is obscure, and although they were referred to by numbers in 1853, the 1859 reference to the green engine suggests that the new engines were not numbered and only known by their colours. This in turn suggests different colours for each engine; but the colours have apparently always been light-green bodywork with black bands lined vermilion on the boilers and brown frames, whilst the domes (where provided) and other mountings were of polished brass except for the chimney caps which were copper.

To add to the confusion, there is a reference to No. 3 in 1860 prior to the delivery of the Slaughter engine which became No. 3. However, it is possible that this was an abbreviation and the reference should have been to the third engine which eventually became No. 4. If the engines were actually numbered around this period, some sort of renumbering was carried out about the time the official No. 3 arrived, but no details have come to light.

Notes based on extracts from the Waterford newspapers, made by Mr K. A. Murray and published in Journal No. 54 of the Irish Railway Record Society.

The *Mars* arrived from Liverpool on 11 May 1853 carrying 'an immense engine—weighing 15 tons!', the first of the three Bury tanks; the next arrived in August, the third in September or October. The Fairbairn tender engine came in April 1854 and had 16 in. x 22 in. cylinders, 5 ft coupled wheels and an estimated 250 h.p. It was (twice) suggested to be a goods engine intended for the Waterford & Limerick Railway; if true, this would mean it was a 2—4—0, but from the WLR records it does not seem possible. It is much more likely to have been the 0—4—2 engine with 15½ in. x 22 in. cylinders which was sold by Dargan to the Limerick & Ennis Railway in 1859, but was not then new, its date being later given as 1856. It lasted till 1900 as WLR No. 2.

The first of the Fairbairn tanks arrived on the *Mars* on 28 April 1855. Four days later it was brought (not, apparently, in steam) by the mid-day train to Tramore. There Mrs Power, wife of the High Sheriff of Waterford 'breaking a bottle of claret on its front, announced its name as *City of Waterford*'. There is no evidence, however, that the engine ever actually carried the name.

# CHAPTER III

# Rolling Stock

The passenger rolling stock was a most interesting and varied collection, but unfortunately the company's records are very incomplete on this aspect and our information is scanty, especially on the original vehicles. As we have seen, only four vehicles were in service on the opening day, and it is possible that these had been brought in by Dargan as the new vehicles ordered had not been delivered. In any case the shortage was soon overcome and in September 1854 one first and two second-class carriages were surplus to requirements and were sold at a profit to the Dublin & Wicklow Railway.

The 1867 Railway Commission Report mentions six first, seven third and one composite coach; the last mentioned had first and third-class compartments and a luggage compartment, while the guard occupied a curious little structure projecting over the buffers at one end, from which he operated the hand brakes.

As far as can be ascertained all the original vehicles were six-wheelers and some of the thirds were open above the waist-line. As the platforms at both Waterford and Tramore were on the western side of the line, some vehicles had the door handles removed on the eastern side and the opens were also closed in on that side.

Several of the firsts were interesting as illustrating the evolution of the railway carriage from the stage coach, each containing three compartments which were decorated externally with a beading following the curved lines of a coach body.

The first-class carriages were painted dark blue with white lining and the third-class dark red (of brownish hue) with black lining. The inside of the frames was painted orange. Lettering was yellow edged with red and the number appeared in a garter bearing the company's name, once on each vehicle. Curiously, the first-class carriages were always marshalled at the Tramore end of the trains. All rolling stock was fitted with side chains and was maintained in spotless condition, one or more vehicles at a time being in the shops for overhaul. Lighting was provided by oil lamps up to 1911 when some vehicles were fitted with acetylene gas.

We are indebted for the following information to Mr R. N. Clements, of the Irish Railway Record Society.

The W & T carriage stock, as it was at the amalgamation and remained until 1933, was a unique collection of which it is only possible to illustrate the most interesting examples. This may have been because many of these spent most of their time under the station roof at Waterford.

It has sometimes been suggested that the 21 carriages handed over to the GSR at amalgamation included all that ever ran on the line, but that was not so. Probably all the first class survived to the end, some converted to third class, but all the original thirds (or rather seconds) of 1853 had been replaced by 1900. The details available are not entirely satisfactory, as the list supplied to the GSR in 1924 was not always reliable; it has been interpreted in the light of various references in the minute books, but it is not always easy to reconcile the two versions.

The first-class carriages were numbered separately from the thirds, which were known as seconds until September 1854, but there were never more than two classes. The numbering of the third brakes in a separate list appears to have been a much later development. Coaches were six-wheeled unless otherwise stated.

No. 1 first, 23 ft 7 in. long, had no date recorded in the list, but it certainly dated back to the opening of the line if, indeed, it was not secondhand even then. Its most interesting feature was the boot in the end coupé compartment which originally contained a folding bed. This coach, built by John Dawson of Dublin, was almost certainly identical with those supplied by him for the opening of the Midland Great Western Railway in 1847. It was a tragedy that it was sold, along with a number of others, in May 1933, and the body was in use as a bungalow at Tramore, though it had apparently disappeared by 1935 (Fig. 28).

No. 2, 24 ft long, is also undated in the list, but was the original No. 2 of 1853, probably also built by Dawson. It too was sold in 1933.

No. 3 was a replacement listed as 1892. It was 27 ft 3 in. long, and was sold in 1933.

No. 4 was bought in 1900 from the Great Southern & Western

Railway, having been built by the Metropolitan Carriage & Wagon Co. in 1878 for the Waterford, Dungarvan & Lismore Railway. Save for being a six-wheeler it was identical with Nos. 9 and 10 firsts. It was sold in 1933.

No. 5, 27 ft 6 in. long, was a replacement supplied in 1877 by Ashbury. It had five compartments and lasted until 1941.

No. 6, the open first class (Fig. 24), is undated in the list. But in 1857 three carriages were ordered from Dawson, one the same as the Kingstown second class, to be marked First Class for this company, to be divided into two compartments, and one step at each door, together with two thirds, and these must have been the three open carriages. Some alterations were made to the design before completion, and this may refer to the division into five compartments instead of two. Probably the coach was originally open both sides, though windows were later provided on the east side. No. 6 was 26 ft. 10 in. long and lasted till 1941, having been converted to third class in 1936.

Nos. 7 and 8, both with five compartments, are listed as 1891. Tenders were taken that year from the Metropolitan Carriage & Wagon Co. for two firsts, but only one is recorded as being ordered. Possibly the order was later increased to two, but the odd thing is that the coaches are not identical, No. 7 being 27 ft 6 in. long and No. 8 28 ft 6 in. Both were converted to third in 1936 and withdrawn in 1937.

Nos. 9 and 10 were 26 ft long and were identical with No. 4 save that they had only four wheels. They were also ex-Waterford, Dungarvan & Lismore stock bought from the GS & WR and were withdrawn in 1941.

No. 1 third was 24 ft long with five compartments and was listed as 1894, but the minutes contain no record of any coach being ordered then. Most likely this was one of the firsts altered to third and 1894 may be the date of alteration. It was sold in 1933.

No. 2 was the same length, but with only four compartments. Listed as 1895, the same comments apply as to the date of No. 1. It was withdrawn in 1937.

No. 3, probably a four-wheeler, was 26 ft 3 in. long with five compartments and seems to have been obtained new as a third in 1892 from the Metropolitan Carriage & Wagon Co. It was withdrawn in 1937.

No. 4 was a four-wheeled, four compartment vehicle, 25 ft long, listed as 1900. This means it was one of the five bought from the GS & WR in that year, of which four were ex-WDLR and one ex-Waterford & Central Ireland Railway. This being the odd one of the five as regards length, was no doubt the WCIR one. It was sold in 1933.

Nos. 5 and 6 were the two open thirds by Dawson, obtained along with No. 6 first in 1857. The order refers to them as having one step at each door and wheels 16 ft centre to centre. Both had six compartments, but they differed in length, No. 5 being 26 ft and No. 6 only 24 ft 7 in. No. 5 was sold in 1933, and No. 6 withdrawn in 1937.

Nos. 7 and 8 thirds did not appear in the 1924 list; these seem to be the original numbers of Nos. 2 and 3 third brakes.

No. 9 was a 26 ft 6 in. six-compartment carriage listed as 1900, but a minute of October 1890 orders that six-compartment first-class carriage No. 4, known as the 'Oak Carriage', should be converted and used as third. As this is the only six-compartment third in the list except the two open carriages, and as its number would correspond to renumbering into the third-class list in 1890-1, no doubt it was the Oak Carriage. Its appearance corresponds with an early date, probably 1853, and it was most likely another of Dawson's build. It originally had doors on both sides, but the door handles on the east side had been removed. The dog box under the seats in the middle of the coach will be noticed (Fig. 25). It was withdrawn in 1937.

No. 10 was 26 ft long with five compartments, listed as 1891, but as 26 ft was the length of the WDLR carriages bought in 1900, of which one remains to be accounted for, it seems that this was it. Assuming the dates of 9 and 10 to have been transposed in the list, 1891 would correspond to the date of conversion of the Oak Carriage to third. No. 10 was withdrawn in 1937.

No. 1 third brake, with two compartments, was supplied by Pickering in 1913 and was sold in 1946, the last carriage obtained by the W & T and the last to remain in service.

No. 2 was 24 ft long with two compartments and No. 3 26 ft 9 in. long with four compartments. No date is recorded for either, which probably indicates that their age was considerable. Both were withdrawn in 1941.

Most of the first-class coaches had lights at the end and between the compartments, while the thirds had only partitions reaching to shoulder height, and were not upholstered.

No automatic brake was ever fitted to any of the W & T stock except for No. 1 third brake obtained in 1913. The Board of Trade regulations were that trains must be capable of being brought to a halt by the hand brakes alone when approaching a terminus. As the only stations on the line were termini, this was interpreted to mean that automatic brakes were not essential.

On the amalgamation in 1925, the only change was the addition of the suffix 'w' to the existing numbers and the renumbering of the brake vans in a separate series. The latter had been done at least nominally before the amalgamation, as they were shown as Nos. 1-3 on the list supplied to the GSR, but No. 1 still bore its old number 12 in 1926. The summer of that year also saw the arrival of an ex-Great Southern & Western third brake.

No further change took place until May 1933, when nine coaches were sold followed by seven more in 1937 and four (including the open first) in 1941. The last passenger vehicle was the third brake, No. 1, which remained in existence until 1946.

The initial withdrawal of the original stock had been occasioned by the delivery on 10 March 1933 of six new vehicles; these were of up-to-date design and had been built in 1928 as steam Clayton bogie-cars. They incorporated such refinements as steam heating, electric light and transverse seating on the back-to-back principle. Apparently the locomotive portions, having been found to be heavy on coal, were removed in 1932 and, in order to save expense, the cars were articulated in pairs and thus required only three new bogies. The bodies were 53 ft 3 in. long, and originally all had a brake compartment next to the engine and a first-class compartment at the far end. But for use on the W & T they were modified as follows :

No. 358    95 third-class seats
No. 359    16 first, 57 third-class seats and a brake compartment
           (probably the original arrangement)
No. 360    16 first and 69 third-class seats
No. 361    85 first-class seats
No. 362    96 third-class seats
No. 363    96 first-class seats

Nos. 359 and 360 were later altered to third class throughout.

At the same time two six-wheeled ex-GS & WR coaches were transferred, an interesting point being that those from this source were altered from oil-gas to acetylene lighting.

As the Clayton cars were vacuum fitted, the engines acquired the necessary apparatus and the W & T stock which ran after 1933 was piped. This enabled the heavy summer traffic to be handled by all available stock while complying with the regulation of the Railway Traffic Act (1889) that the ratio of braked to unbraked stock must be one to four respectively, in the case of trains running 10 miles or less without stopping.

Needless to say, the Clayton cars were the best on the line, and two of them with brake van No. 608 sufficed for the winter traffic.

As can be seen, coaches from many other lines were acquired over the years. The Great Northern Railway was represented by No. 8R mentioned on page 46 and the Midland Great Western was also represented by 56M, a 23 ft four-wheeled parcels van which had sliding doors and was retained for use with the railcars, principally for the conveyance of prams.

### GOODS VEHICLES

The goods traffic was small and mainly confined to coal for the Tramore gasworks which adjoined the east side of the Tramore terminus. There was also a coal factor having a store at the Tramore station. It may be added that the Tramore gasworks finally gave up the ghost in 1935, after electric light had been brought to the town. There was also a small outwards traffic from Tramore in sand for building purposes until the taking of this from the beach at Tramore was prohibited. No separate goods trains were ever run, except perhaps during the period of Government control, although there is no documentary evidence to this effect.

There were originally 10 open goods trucks, reduced to eight by 1867 and finally to five only. At times of pressure, such as the Tramore Races, temporary seats were put in them, and they were used for passenger traffic.

There were also at least three covered wagons of which No. 11W was the last surviving W & T vehicle.

(12) *Exterior Tramore station, 1959*
(13) *Tramore, 1959*
(14) *Tramore, 1960. Note camping coach on right*

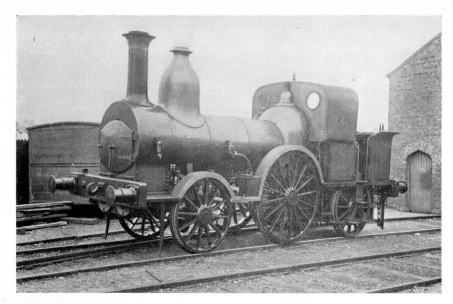

(15) & (16) WTR *old No. 4 ex*-LBR

(17) WTR *No. 4, Bury 1846, taken in 1900 when working*
(18) *A Fairbairn as rebuilt in 1865*

(19) WTR *No. 3 with the two brothers Martley and the head porter at Tramore*

(20) WTR *No. 3* (c.1910)

(21) WTR *No. 4 Barclay*, 1908

# CHAPTER IV

# Description of the Line

The Waterford terminus, known as the Manor station, was in a quiet backwater off Manor Street, in the south-eastern part of the city but quite convenient to the centre; indeed it was closer than Waterford North, which in addition is on the other side of the River Suir. The distance between the two stations is about 1¼ miles.

It was quite a creditable erection for a small line, and consisted of a long single platform stretching north and south for 239 yd, covered by an overall roof for more than half its length. A second line lay through the covered portion and was used for carriage storage, and at the east side was an engine shed ending in a small repair works. Beyond this was the run-round loop; all the lines ended in a small turntable, 22 ft 3 in. diameter, from which some stub sidings, capable of storing a wagon apiece, projected. One longer spur passed out under a gateway to the edge of the curb in Railway Square; this was formerly used for bringing in new rolling stock. A siding off the run-round loop led to a covered carriage shed. It was the rule never to run bunker first on the Tramore line, all engines having to pass over the turntables at each terminus.

At the south end of the station was a level crossing, protected by one of the only two signals on the line. The station building was two-storied, with the manager's office on the first floor, and was described in a local guide as 'built in the Elizabethan style, with cut limestone quoins, window frames, door jambs, etc.' It was double-fronted, and in the left-hand window were two ticket hatches, a third ticket hatch, for use during peak periods, was provided in the curtain wall adjoining the south end of the station.

An interesting feature was the grandfather clock in the entrance hall, surely unique as an official railway timepiece. It was said to have been made by a Waterford clockmaker named Mosely and lasted from the opening to the closing of the line.

The line was single throughout, and was officially (if not invariably) worked by 'a single engine in steam', so no signalling or interlocking was necessary. The scene was almost rural, as the front part of the platform was shaded by trees, and there was little evidence of the bustle of a large town.

Leaving the station, the south suburbs of Waterford were soon passed, and the line traversed a reedy low-lying district that was sometimes under water, interrupting the train service. The gradients were mostly easy, the first two miles being level followed by an upward rise at 1 in 156, 222, 266 and 83 to the summit level $4\frac{1}{4}$ miles from Waterford. Thence the line fell at 1 in 134 for $\frac{3}{4}$ mile, and again at 1 in 140 for $\frac{1}{2}$ mile approaching the Tramore terminus. The district is sparsely populated and the land poor, hence the lack of any intermediate station. For the first two miles the main road to Tramore is on the right of the line, and formerly it switched to the left-hand side over a level crossing. This was altered to an overbridge, on which the W & T spent £700. Two secondary roads were crossed by underbridges, and the halfway point was reached where there was an advertising notice on the right : 'Half Way to Tramore, Hearne & Co., Waterford' (a drapery firm). Here there was for a short time a passing loop only used at time of pressure, such as the race days at Tramore.

The line made a lengthy S curve towards the south-east, and then ran beside the main road, now on the left-hand side, crossing it by an overbridge about a mile from Tramore. It was here that the proposed extension to Dunmore was to start. Just before this point two other secondary roads were crossed by overbridges. The sea did not come into view till just before reaching Tramore. The spire of Tramore Church was visible three miles north of the terminus.

The station was a single-platform building, much like that at Waterford, the lower portion being covered by an overall roof; but only one line ran through the covered portion, which ended in a small turntable, 18 ft diameter. On the east side was a run-round loop and a covered carriage shed. At the northern end was the only other signal on the line, kept at danger and only lowered when a train was approaching and the points to the loop were correctly set. This had to be done *in situ*, and as the signal was some little way from the station the head porter at Tramore got some useful exercise when he had left the job to the last moment. The station building, of two storeys, included a house for the general manager, overlooking the main square at Tramore and quite conveniently situated for the strand.

An old drawing of a proposed station at Tramore depicts this

300 yd further south, with a span roof supported by pillars over a single platform, and a substantial three-storey building adjoining. Fronting this is a roadway, now Strand Street, sweeping round to the left, heavily embanked by stone retaining walls, and continuing down to the adjacent sea shore.

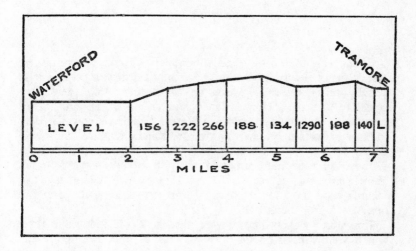

CHAPTER V

# Day to Day Working: Staff

Considering the railway had a monopoly, the fares were moderate; at first they were 8d and 6d first and third class respectively, and 1s and 9d return. However on 13 February 1877 these were raised to 1s and 8d single, 1s 6d and 1s return, at which they remained until the first world war. Return tickets were available on the day of issue only; cheaper afternoon and excursion fares were issued on certain days, including 'bathing' tickets issued from Waterford by the first train at 6d return, third class. From Tramore there were market returs, 9d third class, on Wednesday and Saturdays by the 9.15 a.m. train. These were also available on the first Monday of the month.

The return tickets issued were always of the indivisible type, which were nipped on the forward journey and collected in the carriages on the return, but this did not apply to the tickets issued to other lines; on these, second-class tickets were available first class on the Tramore line.

The starting of the train was made quite a little ceremony, as five minutes before departure a bell was tolled at each terminus, then tickets were examined in every compartment and the doors locked, to be unlocked just before departure. Having made sure that this procedure was completed, the bell was tolled again, the platform gates were closed, the guard sounded his whistle, to be answered from the locomotive by a toot, and finally the train moved slowly out under the respectful gaze of the idlers on the platform. Watching the train go out was then about the only amusement at Tramore on a wet day, and it was tempered by the knowledge that no repeat performance could be expected for nearly two hours.

The maximum speed was limited to 45 m.p.h., and the early railway guides state that the journey took 20 minutes; actually it is believed the official time was 16 minutes.

On Tramore race days and public holidays practically the whole of the rolling stock was made up into one long train, and two engines were then required. Sometimes one would remain at Tramore, merely banking the outgoing trains to the top of the gradient and returning.

The working was certainly unorthodox, as there was no signalling or interlocking, the first train arriving at the passing loop having to wait there till the one in the opposite direction arrived. On one occasion the relief driver on the train from Tramore waited some time at the loop and then decided to proceed to Waterford. However, a company employee who was walking along the main road saw the second train approaching, and was able to signal the drivers and prevent a collision. After this the loop was taken up, and never replaced. At that time the telephone was not invented, and there was no communication between the termini.

The weekday service before 1914 was generally the same, summer and winter alike, but the Sunday service was more frequent in summer. Trains left Waterford on weekdays at 8.30 and 10.45 a.m., and 12.0, 2.0, 4.15, 5.30, 7.20 and 9.0 p.m., and Tramore at 9.10 and 11.15 a.m., and 1.15, 2.50, 4.45, 6.0, 7.50 and 9.30 p.m. About 1911 an additional evening train was put on in each direction. On Sundays nine trains ran in summer and five in winter. Excursions came to Tramore during the summer from inland towns such as Clonmel and Kilkenny, but passengers had to find their own way across Waterford between the stations.

The first manager was Lewis S. Demay, and on the Board were the Hon. Hayes St Leger, Edmund Powell, Henry Massey, Thomas Mackie; the acting secretary was W. Wood, and honorary secretary Edward Dombrain, the son of Sir James Dombrain, the chairman. On 6 May 1855, the *Waterford News* announced the arrival at Tramore of Sir James and Lady Dombrain; bonfires blazed and the station was decorated.

Sir James remained chairman until 1866, and eventually died on 24 September 1871. John Malcolmson was the next chairman, in office from 5 July 1866 until 8 March 1876, when he declined to reconsider his resignation. He was succeeded by Edmund Power who held sway until his death in 1880. His successor was Abraham Denny. The next chairman was G. Morley, who resigned on 31 October 1908, being succeeded by C. E. Denny, who remained in office until the amalgamation.

On the locomotive side, Henry Waugh was locomotive superintendent from 1860 to 1908, when he was just over 80 years of age. He was born in Dublin in May 1827, and served a seven-year apprenticeship with Lamphrey, Rendel & Lamphrey in 1841. After remaining with this firm for a further four years, he went to the Dublin & Drogheda Railway as an engine fitter for three years. As he lived in Dublin he had interesting recollections of the atmospheric railway from Kingstown to Dalkey; he likewise remembered the first locomotives sent to Ireland for the Dublin and Kingstown line, including the *Hibernia*. In 1854 he joined the Waterford & Kilkenny Railway as fitter and engine driver, and four years later was promoted to assistant locomotive superintendent. From this line Waugh transferred to the Waterford & Tramore in 1860.

Tall, with longish beard, he was a fine specimen of a man, and even when over 80 and lame, he retained his energies. As locomotive superintendent of the Tramore line his salary did not exceed £3 5s per week, which he augmented by operating a boot-and-shoe repairing establishment near the station. Some of Waugh's opinions seemed quaint; when the Dublin, Wicklow & Wexford Railway was extended to Waterford in 1904 he thought it would be 'a useful feeder to the Tramore line'. This was in fact quite true, remembering Tramore's position as a holiday resort. It is doubtful if much through traffic originated from the Tramore line although in later years there was a considerable flow to it, especially of excusion traffic. He wanted an electric tramway in Waterford to connect the stations. There was in fact once a scheme for electric tramways.

Retiring from the railway in 1908, he lived only about another year, for on Christmas Day 1909 he was attacked by abdominal pains and in less than 24 hours had died from heart failure and old age, aged 82.

His successor was John Ramsey, who had been the resident fitter for many years, but he died in 1912. He was succeeded by E. G. Johnson, of the Great Southern & Western Railway, who held the office up to the close of the company's independent existence.

The company had no regular engineer, this post being only on a part-time basis, and William Friel, a civil engineer practising at Waterford, held it for many years at the start of the century.

Among the staff worthy of mention was the guard, Patrick Madigan, in resplendent gold-laced uniform, who was described as the most popular guard any railway anywhere ever had, if one excluded his successor, guard Christy Falconer, who only died in April 1957. In the 1890s the usual engine driver was Patrick Martley, assisted by Thomas Alcock as fireman. Both these functionaries wore the round hats fashionable for locomotive staff in those days; they will be noticed in the illustration of engine No. 3 at Tramore (plate 19). Also in this illustration is James Murphy, the head porter at Tramore.

A word may be said here as to the wages of the staff. In 1899 Arthur Prossor, the secretary and manager, was being paid £175 a year, and Henry Waugh's remuneration was about the same. The engine drivers received from 35s to 40s for a seven-day week, and the firemen 24s. John Doyle, the carpenter, received 32s, and Patrick Brett, the permanent way overseer, 30s. Patrick Madigan, the guard, got 25s for a seven-day week, while the porter's wages ranged from 17s to 14s, also for a seven-day week. There were two gangers, on a six-day week, at 16s 6d, and six milesmen at 13s.

These wage scales were comparable with those on other local railways, and the hours worked were from ten to twelve per day. A post in the railway service was not a short cut to fortune, but there was no difficulty in obtaining applicants.

The Wages Schedule for 26 July 1897 shows two ticket collectors and stationmasters, one parcel clerk, one guard, four porters, one gateman, one apprentice, one fitter (Ramsey), one cleaner, one driver, one fireman, one steam raiser (nightman), one cleaner-helper, one helper, one carpenter, one permanent-way overseer, two gangers, and six milesmen, besides the general manager, accountant, and probably a couple of clerks. Including the locomotive superintendent this totals 32, but extras may have been employed at various times.

Another newspaper extract refers to a derailment on 27 August 1954. The practice then was for the engine to be detached from the train when approaching Tramore, after which it ran ahead over the facing points into the siding, the coaches following by gravity into the platform. On this occasion the tender engine was derailed at the points, though whether the coaches then collided with it is not clear. The paper agreed that as the engine was too long for the turntable, this method of working could not be avoided with it, but urged that the practice should be discontinued 'with the old engines which are generally in use'.

# CHAPTER VI

# Accidents

During over 100 years' existence the W & T had only three serious derailments. The first was in 1858 when, on 9 August, the 6.20 p.m. from Tramore crashed through the wall of the Waterford terminus, the two engines hauling the heavy train going right out on the public street. One girl was killed and another injured, but none of the passengers in the train were hurt. Curiously on this occasion the manager was acting as guard.

The other two accidents were in the present century. In 1935 the citizens of both places were shocked by the news of a serious accident involving derailment of part of a train. It occurred on 24 August when the engine of the 12.15 p.m. from Waterford became derailed at Carriglong bridge, and after travelling 300 yd, dragging the coaches after it, went down an embankment at Perry's Bridge. Fortunately Dr Philip Purcell was passing at the time along the nearby roadway, and immediately went to the aid of the injured, who were subsequently removed to the City and County Infirmary, Waterford.

The locomotive was No. 483, a 2—2—2WT built by Fairbairn in 1855, and was in charge of driver Michael Power, with fireman M. Phelan. The guard of the train was the popular Christy Falconer. Power was the more seriously injured, with head and back injuries, while Phelan suffered a broken collar bone and crushed ear. Fortunately, due to Falconer's presence of mind, the accident was not as serious as it might have been; feeling a bump when passing the first bridge, he looked out and finding the train off the road, promptly applied the hand brake and held on to it as hard as he could. As soon as the train stopped, he took immediate steps to get the passengers out as quickly as possible on to the nearby roadway, for fear of an explosion. They paid great tribute to his resourcefulness.

The engine appeared to be extensively damaged, with funnel

detached, body bent and battered and covered with dust and earth. Fortunately, the coaches, including one of the Clayton units, remained standing, which helped to reduce what might have been a very heavy casualty list. It was believed that the lives of the engine crew had been saved owing to the locomotive hitting a telegraph pole. About 1.30 p.m. officials of the GSR arrived on the scene and track repairs were arranged, it being anticipated that normal services could be resumed the following day. It was stated that the engine, the last single and the last Fairbairn running, could be salvaged, and it is understood that Mr Morton, the GSR general manager, had instructed that this should be done. Owing to some misunderstandings, however, it was scrapped.

The cause of the accident was never established. One theory was that a rail had been removed by 'disaffected persons'. There was at this time some unrest among local farmers, and minor outrages on the railways round Waterford had occurred. But the campaign against paying rates had collapsed by this time, and the more likely explanation is buffer locking on the Claytons.

The railway's third derailment was even more startling. At midnight on 4 August 1947, a large number of people on the Strand Road, Tramore, had the shock of seeing a railway engine suddenly shoot through the solid brick wall separating the station from the road and charge out on to the roadway. Broken masonry showered in all directions, and two civic guards (policemen) standing in the roadway had narrow escapes.

The train concerned was the last one from Waterford, which was carrying few passengers, though many were waiting at Tramore for the return journey. On arrival at Tramore the engine, No. 560, failed to stop at its usual place and ran over a turntable and through the wall at the end of the station; fortunately the couplings broke, so the coaches were not seriously involved in the accident. The removal of the engine presented serious difficulties; of course heavy lifting gear, such as breakdown cranes, could not be used, and recourse was needed to the tedious business of jacking up and packing.

In 1953 a little girl fell from a coach of a moving train, but on the whole the W & T was not accident prone; minor troubles occurred occasionally, such as a small fire in a coach and a wagon derailment at the Tramore turntable the same year. Yet throughout the line's entire career only one passenger was killed.

c

CHAPTER VII

# Anecdotes

The late Mr W. E. Jacob, of Waterford and Tramore, who for eleven consecutive years towards the end of the last century travelled on the line to and from school at Waterford, usually behind engine No. 4, related the following:

The first train from Tramore departed at 9.10 a.m., and most of the first-class season-ticket holders had their own particular seats thereon, intruders being greeted with sour looks. One particular compartment was occupied by the Railway Magnates, and known as the 'House of Lords'. In the first place was Mr Arthur Prossor, the secretary and manager of the company, and with him Messrs O'Malley, of the Waterford, Dungarvan & Lismore line, O'Neill of the Waterford & Central Ireland, and Murphy of the Waterford & Limerick Railway. The only outsider admitted to this exclusively railway party was Mr J. H. McGrath, editor and proprietor of the newspaper *The Waterford Citizen*.

At this time Mr Boardman was in charge of the ticket office at Tramore. His son, Harry, became accountant to the company, and later was on the staff of the Great Southern Railways.

The County of Waterford seldom experiences heavy snowstorms, and I can only recollect traffic twice having been interfered with by snow. The first time was in the great blizzard at the end of February 1892. Snow began to fall about midday on a Friday and continued all that day, causing drifts on the line and delaying traffic. After nightfall conditions became worse, and the last train to leave Tramore station did not get as far as the first bridge when it became hopelessly embedded and remained there all night until a relief train from Waterford, having cut a road through the drifts, arrived about noon the next day and pushed the stranded train before it to Tramore. I remember seeing the two trains with their engines coupled head to head coming cautiously into Tramore.

The second time when snow caused trouble was during the very long and bitterly cold winter of 1916-17—the worst fall was not till early in the month of April 1917. Snow fell all one Sunday night, and by Monday morning the drifts were very deep, although it had ceased snowing. There was no sign of the first train from Waterford which was due to leave Tramore on the return journey at 9.10 a.m., but just at that hour an engine appeared without any accompanying carriages, having left Waterford at an early hour and cleared the line of obstructions. There were a few spare carriages at the Tramore end and these were requisitioned to make up a train, so the passengers suffered little inconvenience.

I should mention the method of bringing in new rolling stock to the line. When the Waterford, Dungarvan & Lismore line was amalgamated with the Great Southern & Western in 1898, a number of the old Dungarvan carriages were acquired by the Tramore railway. These were brought from the Waterford terminus of the Dungarvan line through the streets of Waterford, the front pair of wheels resting on a trolley, the rear wheels travelling along the roadway. A team of ten horses was required for the job. (But, as already related, a different method had to be used for engines).

At the time of the Tramore Races the company's carrying capacity would be strained to the utmost. The whole passenger rolling stock would be in use, and open goods trucks would be added, these being provided with temporary wooden seats. Later when some new carriages were purchased, the goods trucks ceased to be used.

The engine driver's name was Waters, an elderly man with a beard. I never saw him without his hat. On the retirement of Waters, Patrick Martley came from the Waterford & Limerick Railway to take his place, with Tom Alcock as fireman and relief driver, and Peter Sullivan sometimes acted as relief as well. There was no stationmaster at either station at this time. The head porter at Tramore was James Murphy. (He appears in the photo of No. 3, plate 19.)

Mr W. E. Jacob had another memory of the Waterford & Tramore Railway. The method used for conveying men and materials for maintenance work on the line was by slipping an open wagon from the rear of a passenger train. He often remembered watching this process as a boy through one of the three small windows at the end of the last carriage on a train from Tramore to Waterford to which the wagon was attached by a plain link coupling.

When approaching the place where the wagon was to be dropped, the engine slowed down so that the coupling would slacken, when the coupling was detached from the carriage drawhook, or possibly from that of the wagon by hooking it up with a shovel. The train then gaining speed again, the wagon would drop behind, to be stopped where required by its brake, which latter may have been lifted from its hook by means of a shovel.

I seem, however, to recollect seeing one of the men perform a sort of circus act by leaning over the wagon side, and applying his weight to the brake lever.

As our house overlooked the railway I had plenty of opportunity of watching the process as operated in the reverse direction, when the engine, on leaving its train in Tramore station, would run back up the line to reappear after some time running in reverse back to the station, pursued down the incline by the wagon, which had presumably been detached by the above method. It was essential that a man should be at the points to divert the wagon on to a siding, where it was stopped by the handbrake.

Another peculiarity of the Waterford & Tramore Railway was that, after leaving the turntable and taking water on the siding, the engine would transfer from the latter to the main road without the aid of a pointsman. The points were normally arranged to leave the main road open to the Tramore station, so that the engine would open the points by means of its wheel flanges, causing the controlling lever to fly back in a truly alarming manner. When the engine had passed over the points, the weighted lever would close them to reopen the road into the station. I do not know when this system was abolished, but it must have been when the platform at Tramore was extended, about the beginning of the present century.

**The late Mr Le Fanu, in his book *Seventy Years of Irish Life*, mentions the following:**

> I was riding on the locomotive (between Tramore and Waterford), when we noticed a small boy of about ten years of age placing a large stone on the line ahead, which he could hardly carry. He then stood back to await results. We pulled up as rapidly as possible, the engine guard dislodging the stone from the track, and gave chase to the boy, whom we soon caught. We brought him back, weeping piteously, and took him up on the engine. He begged us not to kill him; we told him that we would not do this, but intended bringing him to Waterford, where he would be tried, and without doubt, hanged for trying to kill us.

> After half a mile we stopped and released him, and didn't he scamper away! Presumably he feared that we would change our minds and deliver him up to be hanged.

**Some reminiscences of the line appeared in the *Irish Independent* for 5 September 1953, from which these extracts are taken:**

> It seems but yesterday that as a small boy I was commanded to run over to Manor Station and see the time, yet that was 62 years ago. There stood the old grandfather clock, and its ticking echoed throughout the deserted entrance hall. I heard a footstep behind me, and swinging round came face-to-face with the dearest old man I have ever met. His white hair came down beneath his peaked cap, which bore the word 'Guard'. It was none other than the historic personality Ned Kirwan, the renowned and much-loved guard of the line. Always spruce and neat, the dignified figure with the silver buttons and white hair still stands out prominently in my memory.

> About this time a new head porter came to the station, Patrick Madigan; being mindful of his responsibility toward children playing on the premises, he generally ordered us to clear off. (He later became guard.)

> A young fellow named Christy Falconer had a donkey and a nice spring cart, the property of the railway company. He used to carry

luggage and parcels from the Manor to the North station over the
bridge, then the joint property of the Waterford & Limerick and
Waterford & Central Railways.

We small boys liked Christy very much because he allowed us to
ride with him on his journeys, and I recall our extreme satisfaction
when one day we found Christy with a white pony named Snowball.
Snowball served the railway company for many years.

We were all very sad when Christy was promoted to succeed Pat
Madigan as head porter, for the new man who took over Snowball,
Mick Thompson, had not much time for us. Then in course of time,
Christy succeeded Pat Madigan as guard.

All reminiscences would fail if I did not mention Tom Shea. To the
group of small boys who made themselves a general nuisance by
playing in the railway square Tom Shea was a much dreaded man. He
was the under railway porter, a big man with a big voice and a dark
beard. At the sight of Tom we made ourselves scarce, for no sooner did
he catch a glimpse of us than he bellowed 'Get out o' that', and we
beat a very hasty retreat. The only good point about Tom Shea,
according to our boyish minds, was that his wife kept a little brandy-
ball shop at the corner of the railway square.

Memories of the Thursday excursions to Tramore crowd up. How
packed the train was on these occasions, mothers with their children
clinging to them and the old box-type railway carriages packed to
overflowing. One incident stands out; the train had started and had
just passed Hefferman's Gates (so called because one Jim Hefferman
was the gatekeeper), when a mother in our carriage with a baby on
her knees lifted aside her skirt and said 'Ye may come out now', and
three little children scrambled from under the seat. The engine at that
time was driven by an elderly man named Waters and it took half an
hour to make the journey back.

An amusing story is told of an incident which occurred in one
of the third-class carriages; it would appear that an itinerant
musician often travelled on the line, and having given a rendering
in one compartment, climbed over the half-partition into the next.
Unfortunately on one occasion he landed on the shoulders of a
passenger, who greatly resented such treatment, and in less than
no time a free fight was in progress.

During the 1930s special excursions were run to bring the poorer
children of Waterford to the seaside, and on one occasion 2,000
children were marshalled in procession and proceeded to the platform of the Manor station, accompanied by the Mayor and Alder-
men of the City of Waterford. Messrs T. W. Brewer (district
superintendent) and J. J. Healy (stationmaster) were there to super-
vise, and the train, which stretched the entire length of the platform, was in charge of guard Christy Falconer.

The loading of this vast army took place without a hitch and
everything passed off satisfactorily. The children consumed 7,000

packets of sandwiches, 600 lb. of sweets, 400 lb. of cooked meat (boned free of charge by Messrs Henry Denny, the well known Waterford bacon firm), 350 four-lb. loaves of bread, 180 gallons of milk, 10 boxes of apples, 19 cases of oranges, and 400 dozen small bottles of minerals.

---

**Waterford & Tramore Railway.**

No. **15**

## THIRD CLASS—FREE PASS.

*Available from* ........................ *to* ........ ............ .

*Issued to* ............................................... ...... ........

*Signed* ............... ..        ......... ..        ......        ........

*For Conditions see Back.*

# CHAPTER VIII

# Prosperity and Decline

Looking back on the earlier days of the railway, one cannot but be struck by the great spirit of enthusiasm to make Tramore a popular resort and residential area for the citizens of Waterford. Persons building houses there had the material carried free by the railway company; those purchasing houses received a first-class free railway pass available for five years. Combined rail and hotel tickets could also be obtained providing one week's full board and accommodation at the Grand Hotel, Tramore, for the remarkably low figure of two guineas, which included one double journey a day on the railway for seven days.

---

## WATERFORD AND TRAMORE RAILWAY.

### ALTERATION OF TRAINS.

### On and after OCTOBER 1st, 1876.

THE TRAINS WILL RUN AS BELOW:—

### WEEK DAYS.

| DEPARTURE FROM WATERFORD | DEPARTURE FROM TRAMORE |
|---|---|
| PAR.—1st, and 3rd Class. | PAR.—1st, and 3rd Class |
| *8.0, 11.0, 12.15 *2.0, 4.0, 5.30, 7.15, 9.0. | 9.15, *11.30 1.15 3.0, 4.30 °6.0, 7.45, 9.30. |

### SUNDAYS.

| DEPARTURE FROM WATERFORD | DEPARTURE FROM TRAMORE |
|---|---|
| PAR.—1st and 3rd Class, | PAR.—1st, and 3rd Class |
| *8.15, 12.15, 1.30, 2.30, 4.30, 9.0. | 9.15, 12.45, 2.0, 4.0, °6.0, 9.30, |

Those marked thus * are Mail Trains.

FARES. First class Single Ticket ... ... 1s    Return Ticket. ... 1s 2d
Third do do ... ... ... ... 8d    do do ... 10d
Children under three years of age travel free ; over three and under 12 years, Half-price.

☞ Return Tickets are available only on the day they are issued, and are *not transferable.*

Yearly, Half-Yearly, and Monthly Tickets. Terms—can be known on application at Booking Office.

☞ FROM TRAMORE 3rd Class Return Market Tickets are issued on the First Monday in each Month, and every Wednesday and Saturday Morning, by the 9.15, a.m., Up Train, at Single Fare, available for Return by any Train during the day,

Waterford Terminus, Sept. 25, 1876.                    G. N. BAKER, Secretary.

Smoking in any of the Company's Stations or Carriages expresly forbidden.

☞ It is requested that any complaints or irregularity may be immediately reported to the Manager.

The Waterford & Tramore was, for an Irish line, comparatively prosperous throughout its independent existence, and dividends on the ordinary shares had ranged up to 7½ per cent per annum. For the half-year ending 31 December 1867 there was a balance of £1,012 12s 9d, out of which a dividend of 4s was paid on each ordinary share. In the following year, 1868, the receipts from passengers, which numbered 89,626, amounted to £3,435 14s 9d, and the total receipts were £3,968 0s 2d for the second half-year.

In 1869, the passengers numbered 88,004, with receipts of £3,424, and the total receipts were £3,863, the balance available for dividends, after payment on loans, being £1,876, which allowed a dividend of 5s 6d per annum on the ordinary shares for the half-year.

For many years up to 30 June 1912, the *Stock Exchange Year Book* states that dividends of 4 per cent on the first half-year, and 6 per cent on the second had been paid on the ordinary shares, which were looked upon almost as a gilt-edged local investment returning an average of 5 per cent over a long period. But it must be confessed that this result was only obtained from the parsimonious way the line was worked, and the low wages paid to the staff. For instance, in 1879 the railway carried 75,064 first and 97,564 third-class passengers, the total receipts being £5,997 and the working expenses £3,521, or just over 60 per cent, a figure which could certainly not be obtained nowadays.

The circumstances responsible for the railway's decline are well explained by J. C. Conroy in his *History of Railways in Ireland*.

> The First World War started on August 4, 1914, but the Irish railways did not come under Government control until two years later. The same slump in receipts did not take place as in England, though the war prices hit all the companies heavily in their working expenses, and the net receipts were in all cases lower. Towards the end of 1916, before Government control was decided upon, several restrictions were imposed, facilities for excursion traffic being banned.
>
> With the continued rise in prices the Irish railway workers began to demand higher wages, and bonus additions of a few shillings a week had been granted.... Eventually an Order in Council, which placed the Irish railways under Government control, was issued on December 22, 1916. The compensation payable by the Government was to bring the net receipts during control up to the corresponding figure for the year 1913, allowance being made for the increased cost of wages and materials....
>
> The Minister for Transport could order rates and fares to be modified on any controlled undertaking, and the Government proceeded to increase fares eventually to double the pre-ware rate, and at the same time railwaymen's wages were gradually raised during the period of control to about 250 per cent of that obtaining in 1914. An eight-hour

(22) *Fairbairn single No. 1 about* 1900
(23) *The same engine in final condition*

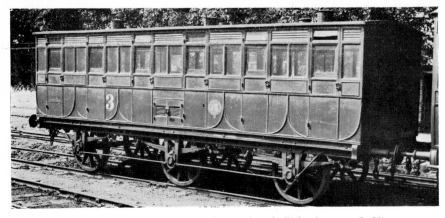

(24) Old WTR *open coach formerly 1st class, built by Dawson, Dublin*
(25) *The closed side of the same coach*
(26) Old WTR *coach with dog compartment, built by Ashburys, Manchester*

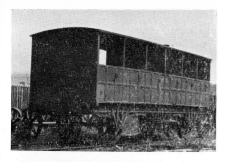
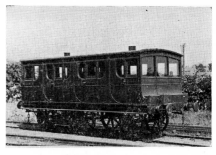
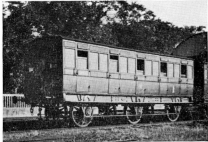

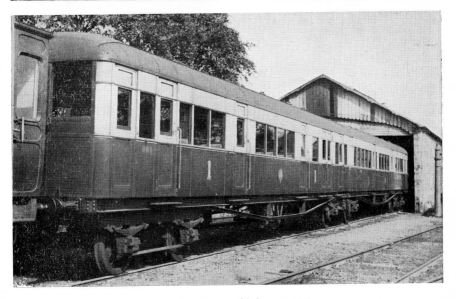

(27) *No. 5 open third, June 1932*
(28) *No. 1 first, June 1932*
(29) *No. 7 first in* GSR *livery*
(30) WTR *covered wagon*
(31) *Two Clayton articulated coaches on Tramore section*

(32) *Accident at Tramore, 4 August 1947*
(33) *Selection of* WTR *tickets*

working day was also introduced.

In July 1921 the Irish railways were faced with the problem of what they were to do when the period of control expired on the 15th of the following month. For five years they had been living under artificial and unnatural conditions. When the British Government took them over it imposed on them practically the same terms of service and expenditure as on the wealthier English railways. As a result the cost of working had increased disproportionately, expenditure had gone up by 250 per cent and receipts by 96 per cent.

The fact that £500,000 of Government compensation money was allotted to the 26 smaller railway companies allowed them to keep going for a short time. But on 28 July 1924 the Government of Ireland passed an Act for the reorganisation of the railways lying wholly within the Irish Free State. All these railways were amalgamated into one company known as the Great Southern Railways on 30 January 1925; and from this date the Waterford & Tramore ceased to be a separate entity.

Apart from the locomotive changes, little was altered and the only new equipment was the transfer of the GS & WR third brake in 1926.

About 1930 the line had to face competition from a bus service known as the Nomad, which brought its passengers right into the centre of Waterford. In 1931 the inhabitants of Waterford and Tramore were greatly perturbed by a report that the GSR proposed to close the railway or else curtail the service. A lengthy petition was organised for presentation to the Minister for Internal Affairs at Dublin. The main points covered were:

1. That the Waterford & Tramore had always been a very prosperous concern, paying dividends up to 7½ per cent.

2. That at the time of its amalgamation with the Great Southern Railways a large reserve had been accumulated from surplus profits, as a result of which shareholders were granted one-fourth more shares in the amalgamated concern than they had held in the original company.

3. It had been estimated that the past year's working had brought a profit of more than £1,000.

4. That closure of the line would inflict great hardship on the general public and business community, as well as the poor of Waterford, who used the line as a convenient means of reaching the seaside.

5. That blunders made in the management of the line by the GSR had hindered the prosperity of the line and alienated public support at a time when bus competition should have been combated.

6.   And, finally, the petitioners prayed 'that any undue curtailment of the service, or closing of the railway line to the public, should not be sanctioned'.

In 1932 the Government passed an Act restricting private bus services, by which the Great Southern Railways bought out the Nomad bus service. But matters continued to deteriorate, so that in 1934 the inhabitants of the districts served travelled to Dublin to put their case before the GSR management. This alarm abated. and the line continued to function as before.

Six Clayton coaches arrived on 10 March 1933 and the first withdrawals of the original coaches took place in May, eliminating all those that had not been piped.

In consonance with the requirements of the Regulation of Railway Traffic Act (1889), which provided that the ratio of braked to unbraked stock must be one to four respectively, on trains running ten miles or less without a stop, it was decided to marshal the stock in the following order for the heavy summer traffic : van No. 1W, fully braked, 24 seats; three coaches, tubed only, 180 seats; six Clayton coaches, fully braked, 516 seats; three coaches, tubed only, 168 seats; one third-class coach, fully braked, 72 seats; two coaches, tubed only, 132 seats; one van No. 608, fully braked, 48 seats; total 17 vehicles with 1,140 seats, comprising 421 first-class and 715 third-class seats. For the winter service Clayton coaches Nos. 358-9 and van No. 608 sufficed.

A trial trip was made over the line, exhibiting the remarkable spectacle of two of the articulated units being hauled by one of the 1855 2—2—2 WTs, halting at the bridges to test the clearances.

The service was increased to a maximum of 14 trains in each direction, with a running time of 15 minutes; due to smart turnrounds at the termini, a train could now follow at 45 minutes interval. The first train from Tramore was now at 8.25 a.m., and the last at 11.30 p.m.

During the Second World War, the roof covering the Manor station became unsafe, and it was therefore removed, the station being left entirely open. A new starting signal was also installed at the end of the platform, in addition to the existing signal on the other side of the level crossing.

# CHAPTER IX

# The Closing Years

The season at Tramore is a short one, usually closing on 15 August; while large numbers of passengers travelled during the summer, for about nine months of the year the traffic was hardly profitable. The *Waterford News* of 20 June 1952 carried an unofficial report that diesel railcars were to be introduced for use during slack hours.

Meanwhile representations were being made by the Mayor of Waterford to Coras Iompair Eireann (as the former Great Southern Railways was now designated) to have a cheap fare introduced during the summer period. The ordinary return was then 2s, but on 14 July 1952 a special fare of 1s return for adults and 6d for children, available on Monday and Wednesday afternoons during the summer, was inaugurated. It may be mentioned that on the previous Sunday night, the 7.30 p.m. train from Waterford carried 1,300 passengers, a record for the year.

On 25 July the *Waterford News* commented on the amazing success of the new cheap fares on Mondays and Wednesdays, and considered that if other railways were to reduce their fares to the level of the public's present capacity to pay, queues would be seen waiting to board the trains.

On 8 August an announcement appeared in the Waterford newspapers of a special train to be run on the 14th at 4 a.m. from Tramore, in connection with a dance to be held in a local hotel, and afterwards a number of similarly chartered trains were run in the early morning for local functions.

Fourteen trains were running every day in each direction in 1953, the line being 'alive' for 17 hours out of the 24. All traffic records for the first fortnight in August went by the board. August 15 was on a Saturday, a broiling hot day, and during the three days, Friday, Saturday and Sunday, it seemed as if every man, woman and child left Waterford city and travelled to Tramore by train. All three engines and every coach were in use and the crowds were packed into every compartment like sardines.

'Not all the buses in Ireland would handle the weekend traffic we had here during August,' commented Guard M. Colbert, then the employee with the longest service. The other veterans of the Tramore railway were Guard Bergin, of Tramore, and Guard Christy Falconer, already alluded to.

Before the end of 1953 the Waterford & Tramore Railway completed 100 years of service to its two communities. The centenary was on 5 September, and despite the absence of official ceremony or of decorations, the staff were much aware of the momentous occasion. Both the *Irish Independent* and the *Waterford News* during the week carried news items and an article in connection therewith. One of the authors, Mr Newham, was at the Manor station for the centenary, and was privileged to travel on, and fire, the engine (No. 555) of the 11.45 a.m. train to Tramore and back.

At this time, the best rolling stock on the line consisted of three units of articulated ex-Clayton railcars. There was also an assortment of old six-wheel coaches, including 8R, a veteran of the Cork & Macroom Direct Railway (originally GNR and later purchased by the CMDR), and 24B, an ex-Cork, Bandon & South Coast Railway coach.

By the end of the year it was announced by CIE that steam traction on the line was to be replaced with diesel railcars; these arrived at Waterford for transhipment in September 1954. Meanwhile the steam trains continued to carry their heavy loads during the summer, and on two trains alone 2,800 passengers travelled to Tramore. On 8 November the railcars Nos. 2658/9 were installed on the Tramore section, though not actually in service. The method of transference has already been described, but in this case the railcars were too long to use the turntable at the end of the Manor station. A special siding was put down at the end of Bath Street level crossing, on to which the vehicles were unloaded from the road bogies. The railcars were second-class only with bus-type seats; 2658 had 80 seats and a brake compartment, and 2659 had no brake compartment and 92 seats.

The end of steam traction came suddenly and unexpectedly in November, when one of the engines drawing a train broke down; this resulted in one of the railcars being put into service, and thus the days of steam haulage were over, and trains became one class only.

Two months previously the old engine shed at the Manor station was dismantled, a small portion being left, to which was joined a long wooden shed for diesel car servicing. When the 1955 summer arrived it was found that the railcars provided insufficient accommodation, and following strong representations from the Corporation of Waterford to the general manager of CIE supplementary bus services were provided at peak periods between Waterford and Tramore. In June another railcar, 2657, arrived together with two Park Royal coaches of which 1407 was given extra luggage space and 1408 was fitted as a driving trailer. All three had bus-type seats.

The company had now transferred three railcars with trailers to the section, and a special van had also to be provided for perambulators, etc., it being the custom among working folk of Waterford to bring these with them when having a day out at Tramore. It is interesting that in the days when the line was an independent entity such vehicles were conveyed free of charge.

Meanwhile the turntables at Waterford and Tramore had been removed and the second road through the former covered portion at Waterford had gone too. The three former steam locomotives were left lying on a siding at the Manor station for some months, but were later removed with a view to being scrapped.

It was soon apparent that the company intended to close the railway and transfer all traffic to the road, and with the coming of the winter season of 1955 the booking offices at Waterford and Tramore were closed, square paper tickets being issued by the guard prior to the departure of the trains. These tickets had a counterfoil portion which was retained by the ticket collector at the station. The booking offices were, however, reopened during the busy hours of the day and all the time during summer.

On 27 September 1960, CIE announced sweeping closure proposals which embraced the Waterford & Tramore section; the Tramore line had frequently carried capacity loadings during the summer, and on one Sunday had been unable to cope with all the traffic offering. But as already stated, the season at Tramore is short. Furthermore, the operation of a small detached section such as this involved CIE in disproportionate expense, and the substitute bus service brought passengers to the centre of Waterford. As CIE was now bound to balance its accounts within a short time, the closure was perhaps unavoidable, however much it was to be regretted.

Considerable local opposition was inevitable, but no amount of public protest would alter the decision, and on 31 December 1960 the line was closed for good. To avoid demonstrations, the last scheduled trains did not run, buses being substituted. The final trains were the 1.25 p.m. from Waterford and the 2.15 p.m. from Tramore. Later in the day the railcars ran light to Tramore to bring in the camping coaches, H.C. 7 & 8, which had only been sent there that spring. Lifting began within a couple of days and was completed by May 1961, the last of the rolling stock being removed on 18 March 1961.

The charges on the substitute bus service, 1s 7d single and 2s 8d day return, were so greatly resented by the residents of Tramore that they formed the 'Tramore Workers Association' which, in return for an 8s 6d per week subscription, permitted members to use a hired bus to and from Waterford for four single journeys a day. This compared with the CIE charge of 11s 9d for similar transportation.

The Waterford & Tramore Railway, though only 7¼ miles long, possessed features of great interest to the railway enthusiast, and served its patrons well for 106 years. Furthermore, unlike most of the small Irish lines, it had been a paying proposition during a considerable portion of its life, though, as already mentioned, it was run on very parsimonious lines. The reckless increase in wages that took place during Government control, and also the drawback of its rather remote terminus at Waterford, may be said to have sealed its fate. Now that the line has gone, Tramore would no longer have the same interest for the authors as it used to have during its existence.

ADDITIONAL NOTES

One might think that in 1925 Inchicore would have had so many urgent problems to deal with that the WTR would have been overlooked for a while, but that was not so. As early as 5 January 1925 a drawing was made for a new built-up crank axle for the single tank No. 1. The lack of continuous brakes was next considered, but was a more difficult question than first appears. An independent steam brake can be graduated as required by the driver, but this did not apply to the combination brake standard on the GSR, in which application of the vacuum resulted in the steam brake (unless pegged) being fully on, so there would be a danger of locking the wheels of a light single-driver engine. This would be the reason for the drawing of March 1925 for the replacement of the steam brake by vacuum on the engine, but another snag arose here. There was no room for fitting a vacuum cylinder, so the proposal was to make a place for it under the bunker by removing the well tank and fitting side tanks, which also involved widening the platforms of the engines. The water capacity would have been increased from 300 to 800 gallons, and engine weight increased by 2½ to 3 tons.

Probably the considerable expense of this job was the reason why

nothing was done, other than the transfer of third brake No. 608 to the
WT section. This, though it had been for many years in GSWR stock,
had a more interesting origin, for it was one of the two passenger
vehicles owned by the Waterford & Wexford Railway in its independent years, 1894-8. In July 1927, however, an empty carriage train
approaching Waterford got out of control due to failure of the engine
brake, and it was then recommended that a certain number of six-
wheel vacuum-fitted vehicles should be transferred to the WT section,
the other coaches piped, and the engines vacuum fitted at a cost of
£200. No immediate action was taken, but vacuum ejectors (retaining
the steam brakes) were fitted to the engines probably in 1929, and
piping of the coaches begun.

The gate referred to on page 27 was put in by the GSR for the transfer of coach No. 608 in 1926. In WT days, arrival of additions to the
rolling stock being rare events, the practice had been to break down
the boundary wall as required and rebuild it afterwards. About the
same time as this coach came, two GSWR open wagons, and possibly a
covered wagon too, were brought over.

It is not quite certain which was the last WT vehicle in service. After
the body of No. 1 third brake was sold in 1946 its underframe was
used, close-coupled with a similar one from the Bandon section, as a
motor-carrier at Rosslare Harbour, and it may perhaps have outlasted
wagon 11W. This was probably the only WT vehicle transferred away
from the line since the sale of three carriages to the DWWR in 1854.